WOOD GASIFICATION SYSTEM

Learn the Off Grid System to Make Fuel, Power and Energy Using the Wood Gasifier

ASHTON WALLING

Table of Contents

Introduction

Gasification is a process that converts organic or fossil based carbonaceous materials into carbon monoxide, hydrogen and carbon dioxide. This is achieved by reacting the material at high temperatures (>700 °C), without combustion, with a controlled amount of oxygen and/or steam. The resulting gas mixture is called syngas which is itself a fuel. The power derived from gasification and combustion of the resultant gas is considered to be a source of renewable energy if the gasified compounds were obtained from biomass.

In a gasifier, the carbonaceous material undergoes several different processes: The dehydration or drying process occurs at around 100°C. The pyrolysis (or de-volatilization) process occurs at around 200-300°C. Volatiles are released and char is produced, resulting in up to 70% weight loss for coal. The combustion occurs as the volatile products and some of the char reacts with oxygen to primarily form carbon dioxide and small amounts of carbon monoxide, which provides heat for the subsequent gasification reactions. The gasification process occurs as the char reacts with carbon and steam to produce carbon monoxide and hydrogen. In addition, the reversible gas phase water gas shift reaction reaches equilibrium very fast at the temperatures in a gasifier. This balances the concentrations of carbon monoxide, steam, carbon dioxide and hydrogen.

In essence, a limited amount of oxygen or air is introduced into the reactor to allow some of the organic material to be "burned" to produce carbon monoxide and energy, which drives a second reaction that converts further organic material to hydrogen and additional carbon dioxide. Further reactions occur when the formed carbon monoxide and residual water from the organic material react to form methane and excess carbon dioxide. This third reaction occurs more abundantly in reactors that increase the residence time of the reactive gases and organic materials, as well as heat and pressure. Catalysts are used in more sophisticated reactors to improve reaction rates, thus moving the system closer to the reaction equilibrium for a fixed residence time.

The choice of feedstock determines the gasifier design. Three designs are common in wood gasification: updraft, downdraft and crossdraft. In an updraft gasifier, wood enters the gasification chamber from above, falls onto a grate and forms a fuel pile.

Air enters from below the grate and flows up through the fuel pile. The syngas, also known as producer gas in biomass circles, exits the top of the chamber. In downdraftor crossdraft gasifiers, the air and syngas may enter and exit at different locations.

CHAPTER 1

Gasification

Gasification is a technological process that can convert any carbonaceous (carbon-based) raw material such as coal into fuel gas, also known as synthesis gas (syngas for short). Gasification occurs in a gasifier, generally a high temperature/pressure vessel where oxygen (or air) and steam are directly contacted with the coal or other feed material causing a series of chemical reactions to occur that convert the feed to syngas and ash/slag (mineral residues). Syngas is so called because of its history as an intermediate in the production of synthetic natural gas.

Composed primarily of the colorless, odorless, highly flammable gases carbon monoxide (CO) and hydrogen (H2), syngas has a variety of uses. The syngas can be further converted (or shifted) to nothing but hydrogen and carbon dioxide (CO2) by adding steam and reacting over a catalyst in a water-gas-shift reactor. When hydrogen is burned, it creates nothing but heat and water, resulting in the ability to create electricity with no carbon dioxide in the exhaust gases. Furthermore, hydrogen made from coal or other solid fuels can be used to refine oil, or to make products such as ammonia and fertilizer.

More importantly, hydrogen enriched syngas can be used to make gasoline and diesel fuel. Polygeneration plants that produce multiple products are uniquely possible with gasification technologies. Carbon dioxide can be efficiently captured from syngas, preventing its greenhouse gas emission to the atmosphere and enabling its utilization (such as for Enhanced Oil Recovery) or safe storage.

Gasification offers an alternative to more established ways of converting feedstocks like coal, biomass, and some waste streams into electricity and other useful products. The advantages of gasification in specific applications and conditions, particularly in clean generation of electricity from coal, may make it an increasingly important part of the world's energy and industrial markets. The stable price and abundant supply of coal throughout the world makes it the main feedstock option for gasification technologies going forward.

The technology's placement markets with respect to many techno-economic and political factors, including costs, reliability, availability and maintainability (RAM), environmental considerations, efficiency, feedstock and product flexibility, national energy security, public and government perception and policy, and infrastructure will determine whether or not gasification realizes its full market potential.

Fundamentals of Gasification

Gasification is a partial oxidation process. The term partial oxidation is a relative term which simply means that less oxygen is used in gasification than would be required for combustion (i.e., burning or complete oxidation) of the same amount of fuel.

Gasification typically uses only 25 to 40 percent of the theoretical oxidant (either pure oxygen or air) to generate enough heat to gasify the remaining unoxidized fuel, producing syngas. The major combustible products of gasification are carbon monoxide (CO) and hydrogen (H2), with only a minor amount of the carbon completely oxidized to carbon dioxide (CO2) and water. The heat released by partial oxidation provides most of the energy needed to break up the chemical bonds in the feedstock, to drive the other endothermic gasification reactions, and to increase the temperature of the final gasification products.

Reactions & Transformations in Gasification

The chemistry of gasification is quite complex and is accomplished through a series of physical transformations and chemical reactions within the gasifier. Some of the major chemical reactions are shown in the diagram below. In a gasifier, the carbonaceous feedstock undergoes several different processes and/or reactions:

- **Dehydration** – Any free water content of the feedstock evaporates, leaving dry material and evolving water vapor which may enter into later chemical reactions.

- **Pyrolysis** – This occurs as the feedstock is exposed to rising temperature in the gasifier. Devolatization and breaking of the weaker chemical bonds occurs, releasing volatile gases such as tar vapors, methane, and hydrogen, along with producing a high molecular weight char which will undergo gasification reactions.

- **Combustion** – The volatile products and some of the char react with limited oxygen to form carbon dioxide (CO2), carbon monoxide (CO), and in doing so, provide the heat needed for subsequent gasification reactions.

- **Gasification –** The remaining char reacts with CO2 and steam to produce CO and hydrogen (H2).

- **Water-gas-shift and methanation –** These are separate reversible gas phase reactions taking place simultaneously based on gasifier conditions. These are minor reactions which play a small role within in the gasifier. Depending on the desired product, the syngas may undergo further water-gas shift and methanation processing downstream from the gasifiers.

CHAPTER 2

Wood Gasification

Wood gas, also called "holzgas", air gas or blue gas, is the product of thermally gasifying a biomass material. Wood gas is generated in a high temperature chemical reaction (>700°) between the wood and a limited amount of steam or oxygen. The heat and lack of oxygen causes the gases in the wood to release in the form of carbon monoxide, hydrogen and carbon dioxide. Boilers pull the wood gas mixture that is created in the upper wood loading chamber into the lower combustion chamber and burn it at temperatures around 2000°.

After the gas is burned, any left over emissions exit through the chimney flue. The most notable indicator of effective gasification is the lack of smoke exiting the chimney. Wood as a fuel is a good solution due to the fact that it is a renewable resource like solar, water or wind power.

Tips for using wood as a fuel:

- Best humidity for wood gasification is 20% in Vedolux boilers
- Most desirable humidity takes about 12-18 months of storing

Composition of Wood Gas

- 51% Nitrogen (N2)
- 22% Carbon Monoxide (CO)
- 18% Hydrogen (H2)
- 6% Carbon Dioxide (CO2)
- 3% Methane (CH4)

CHAPTER 3

How Gasification Works

Some of the most promising, attention-getting energy alternatives aren't revolutionary ideas. We all know about windmills and waterwheels, which have been around for centuries. Today, a variety of improvements, including innovative turbine designs, are transforming these ancient machines into cutting-edge technologies that can help nations satisfy their energy needs.

There's another old process -- one you probably don't know much about -- that's gaining in popularity and may join wind and hydropower in the pantheon of clean, renewable energy. The process is known as gasification, a set of chemical reactions that uses limited oxygen to convert a carbon-containing feedstock into a synthetic gas, or syngas.

It sounds like combustion, but it's not. Combustion uses an abundance of oxygen to produce heat and light by burning. Gasification uses only a tiny amount of oxygen, which is combined with steam and cooked under intense pressure. This initiates a series of reactions that produces a gaseous mixture composed primarily of carbon monoxide and hydrogen. This syngas can be burned directly or used as a starting point to manufacture fertilizers, pure hydrogen, methane or liquid transportation fuels.

Believe it or not, gasification has been around for decades. Scottish engineer William Murdoch gets credit for developing the basic process. In the late 1790s, using coal as a feedstock, he produced syngas in sufficient quantity to light his home. Eventually, cities in Europe and America began using syngas -- or "town gas" as it was known then -- to light city streets and homes.

Eventually, natural gas and electricity generated from coal-burning power plants replaced town gas as the preferred source of heat and light.

Today, with a global climate crisis looming on the horizon and power-hungry nations on the hunt for alternative energy sources, gasification is making a comeback.

The Gasification Technologies Council expects world gasification capacity to grow by more than 70 percent by 2015. Much of that growth will occur in Asia, driven by rapid development in China and India. But the United States is embracing gasification, as well.

Let's take a closer look at how this process works. We're going to start with coal gasification, the most common form of the process.

Coal Gasification

The state believes the area contamination was caused by the Fall River Gas Co. dumping coal gasification waste for decades.

The heart of a coal-fired power plant is a boiler, in which coal is burned by combustion to turn water into steam. The following equation shows what burning coal looks like chemically:

$$C + O_2 \dashrightarrow CO_2$$

Coal isn't made of pure carbon, but of carbon bound to many other elements. Still, coal's carbon content is high, and it's the carbon that combines with oxygen in combustion to produce carbon dioxide, the major culprit in global warming. Other byproducts of coal combustion include sulfur oxides, nitrogen oxides, mercury and naturally occurring radioactive materials.

The heart of a power plant that incorporates gasification isn't a boiler, but a gasifier, a cylindrical pressure vessel about 40 feet (12 meters) high by 13 feet (4 meters) across.

Feedstocks enter the gasifier at the top, while steam and oxygen enter from below. Any kind of carbon-containing material can be a feedstock, but coal gasification, of course, requires coal. A typical gasification plant could use 16,000 tons (14,515 metric tons) of lignite, a brownish type of coal, daily.

A gasifier operates at higher temperatures and pressures than a coal boiler -- about 2,600 degrees Fahrenheit (1,427 degrees Celsius) and 1,000 pounds per square inch (6,895 kilopascals), respectively. This causes the coal to undergo different chemical reactions.

First, partial oxidation of the coal's carbon releases heat that helps feed the gasification reactions. The first of these is pyrolysis, which occurs as coal's volatile matter degrades into several gases, leaving behind char, a charcoal-like substance. Then, reduction reactions transform the remaining carbon in the char to a gaseous mixture known as syngas.

Carbon monoxide and hydrogen are the two primary components of syngas. During a process known as gas cleanup, the raw syngas runs through a cooling chamber that can be used to separate the various components.

Cleaning can remove harmful impurities, including sulfur, mercury and unconverted carbon. Even carbon dioxide can be pulled out of the gas and either stored underground or used in ammonia or methanol production.

That leaves pure hydrogen and carbon monoxide, which can be combusted cleanly in gas turbines to produce electricity. Or, some power plants convert the syngas to natural gas by passing the cleaned gas over a nickel catalyst, causing carbon monoxide and carbon dioxide to react with free hydrogen to form methane. This "substitute natural gas" behaves like regular natural gas and can be used to generate electricity or heat homes and businesses.

But if coal is unavailable, gasification is still possible. All you need is some wood.

Syngas Seconds

Although the electric power industry has recently become interested in gasification, the chemical, refining and fertilizer industries have been using the process for decades. That's because the major components of syngas; hydrogen and carbon monoxide, are the basic building blocks of several other products. Some of the most important products derived from syngas include methanol, nitrogen-based fertilizers and hydrogen for oil refining and transportation fuels.

Even slag, a glasslike byproduct of the gasification process, can be used in roofing materials or as a roadbed material.

Wood Gasification

Coal gasification is sometimes called "clean coal" because it can be used to generate electricity without belching toxins and carbon dioxide into the atmosphere. But it's still based on a nonrenewable fossil fuel. And it still requires mining operations that scar the Earth and leave behind toxic wastes of their own.

Wood gasification or biomass gasification, to be more technically correct may provide a viable alternative.

Biomass is considered a renewable energy source because it's made from organic materials, such as trees, crops and even garbage.

Biomass gasification works just like coal gasification: A feedstock enters a gasifier, which cooks the carbon-containing material in a low-oxygen environment to produce syngas. Feedstocks generally fall into one of four categories:

- Agricultural residues are left after farmers harvest a commodity crop. They include wheat, alfalfa, bean or barley straw and corn stover. Wheat straw and corn remnants make up the majority of this biomass.
- Energy crops are grown solely for use as feedstocks. They include hybrid poplar and willow trees, as well as switchgrass, a native, fast-growing prairie grass.

- Forestry residues include any biomass left behind after timber harvesting. Deadwood works well, too, as do scraps from debarking and limb-removal operations.

- Urban wood waste refers to construction waste and demolition debris that would otherwise end up in a landfill. Pallets -- flat transport structures -- also fall into this category.

The choice of feedstock determines the gasifier design. Three designs are common in biomass gasification: updraft, downdraft and crossdraft. In an updraft gasifier, wood enters the gasification chamber from above, falls onto a grate and forms a fuel pile. Air enters from below the grate and flows up through the fuel pile. The syngas, also known as producer gas in biomass circles, exits the top of the chamber. In downdraft or crossdraft gasifiers, the air and syngas may enter and exit at different locations.

The choice of fuel and gasifier design affects the relative proportions of compounds in the syngas. For example, wheat straw placed in a downdraft gasifier produces the following:

- 17 to 19 percent hydrogen gas
- 14 to 17 percent carbon monoxide
- 11 to 14 percent carbon dioxide
- Virtually no methane

But charcoal placed in a downdraft gasifier produces the following:

- 28 to 31 percent carbon monoxide
- 5 to 10 percent hydrogen gas
- 1 to 2 percent carbon dioxide
- 1 to 2 percent methane

Now you're ready to make your own wood gasifier.

Better Gas(ification) Mileage

Believe it or not, one of the main uses of wood gasification has been to power internal combustion engines. Before 1940, gasification-powered cars were occasionally seen, especially in Europe. Then, during World War II, petroleum shortages forced people to think about alternatives. The transportation industries of Western Europe relied on wood gasification to power vehicles and ensure that food and other important materials made it to consumers.

After the war, as gas and oil became widely available, gasification was largely forgotten. A future petroleum shortage, however, may revitalize our interest in this old technology. The car driver of the future may ask to "fill 'er up" with a few sticks of wood instead of a few gallons of gas.

Homemade Gasification

Does the future hold a lot more energy from gasifiers such as this one?

One attractive quality of gasification is its scalability. The Polk Power Station just southeast of Tampa is a gasification plant covering 4,300 acres (1,740 hectares). It converts 100 tons (90.7 metric tons) of coal an hour into 250 million watts of power for about 60,000 homes and businesses.

But you don't have to be a giant public utility to experiment with gasification. You can build a simple, small gasifier with materials you find around the house.

YouTube features several videos of these homemade units. One video, for example, shows a paint can playing the role of the pressure vessel in which gasification reactions occur. As the syngas is produced inside the sealed can, it moves through some simple plumbing fittings to a burner can, where the gas can be ignited.

Another interesting video shows a small team assembling and operating a wood gasifier based on plans prepared by the U.S. Federal Emergency Management Agency (FEMA) and the Oak Ridge National Laboratory. FEMA developed these plans in 1989 specifically for small-scale gasification in the event of a petroleum emergency. The agency's report includes detailed, illustrated instructions for the fabrication, installation and operation of a downdraft biomass gasifier.

The unit requires a galvanized metal trash can, a small metal drum, common plumbing fittings and a stainless steel mixing bowl and can be mounted on a vehicle to provide syngas for internal combustion. With the gasifier in place, the vehicle can run reliably using wood chips or other biomass as the fuel.

If you're interested in gasification, but aren't the do-it-yourself type, then you might want to consider buying a gasification unit from a manufacturer. For example, New Horizon Corporation distributes gasification systems that can be installed in a home environment. These biomass gasification boilers can heat houses, garages and other buildings and can use a variety of fuels, including seasoned wood, corn cobs, sawdust, wood chips and any kind of pellet.

Either way, gasification will likely emerge as one of the most important energy alternatives in the coming decades. It's the cleanest way to use coal, but also works efficiently with renewable energy sources, such as biomass. And, because one of the primary products of gasification is hydrogen, the process offers a stepping stone to producing large quantities of hydrogen for fuel cells and cleaner fuels.

CHAPTER 4

The Efficient Way to Burn Wood

Properly dried and burned wood is an excellent green fuel for rural heating. Since freshly cut wood may be 60 percent water, the key to minimizing wood cutting, splitting and stacking is to let it dry for at least a year. If you don't, about 40 percent of your wood is burned just to drive off water – no heat results. Most stoves burn with 40 to 60 percent efficiency, and outdoor wood boilers usually get 30 to 50 percent, while a wood gasifier gets 80 to 92 percent – but the key is dry wood. After a year, wood moisture content may be 20 to 35 percent; after two years, 10 to 20 percent.

My gasifier calls for 15 to 25 percent moisture for maximum efficiency, so I dry wood for two years and recently completed a solar wood dryer to try to cut drying time.

With gasification, wood is burned initially in a conventional firebox, then gases are directed to a ceramic combustion chamber where temperatures reach 1,800 to 2,000 F.

All gases and tars are burned, no smoke comes from the chimney and the chimney stays clean. Despite the high gasification chamber temperatures, by the time the gases pass through the boiler's fire-tube heat exchanger, flue temperatures may hit 350 F. My flue temperatures are usually under 250, indicating the efficiency of the fire tube heat exchanger. If wood is too wet, the fire is cooled and white steam exits the chimney. Since wood gasification boilers are mass produced in Europe, they are much cheaper than domestic models. Mine was made in Poland.

I now heat my 1,400-square-foot house, basement and domestic water from fall until late spring on about 3-1/2 cords. Before installing the boiler, my house was 1,000 square feet, and with a wood stove for heat, I burned 3-1/2 cords plus 150 to 200 gallons of oil for domestic hot water.

In cold weather I build one fire a day and keep it going for about eight hours. The key to efficiency is dry wood and a hot, fast burn. My small, 85,000 BTU boiler heats water stored in a 500-gallon propane tank, and this water circulates, on demand, to heat living spaces and domestic water. With year-old wood, my tank reached a maximum temperature of 170 degrees, but with really dry wood, it gets to 180, which greatly increases the BTUs. One fire is good for a day during Maine winters but has lasted for two to three days in the mild fall of 2015. With oil prices down, I burned oil rather than wood in the summer; one fire might supply domestic hot water for a week, but a lot of tank heat would be lost to the basement. A large family taking many showers and doing much laundry would likely benefit from a weekly burn.

Wood is the ideal fuel for rural heating in Maine, especially if you own a woodlot. Firewood harvests are an opportunity to improve the forest by removing dead, dying, diseased and poorly formed trees, enabling residual trees to grow faster, produce more oxygen and use more CO2 greenhouse gases. If you are a gardener, wood ash adds calcium, potassium, other nutrients and bio-char to the soil (but apply only after and according to recommendations of a soil test, as wood ashes can raise the soil pH quickly and excessively). From the energy standpoint, buying wood from a local supplier is far better than buying pellets from afar and minimizes consumption of motor fuels. It also provides local employment and keeps money in the local economy.

I cut about half of my wood from a tiny woodlot and use tops and branches to about 1-1/2 inches in diameter for my kitchen cook stove. Branches and wood under 4 inches are efficiently bucked in a "cutting crib" made several years ago by a friend.

CHAPTER 5

Application of Gasifier

Gasification is a process of conversion of the fuel or organic wastes/matter into a gas called producer gas. This process involves a sequence of chemical and thermal reactions like the oxidation and reduction. The producer gas also called syngas has a calorific value ranging from 1000 to 1200 kcal/Nm3. Other products include gases, tar, charcoal and many more. The products obtained from the gasification process are the primary gases. The names of these gases can be syngas, generator gas, wood gas, coal gas or others. Generally, named as biogas.

Gasification is one form of combustion, i.e. incomplete or choked combustion. The process takes place in the reactor called gasifier at high temperatures in presence or absence of oxygen. Later, the unburnt gases are moved out to burn elsewhere.

Gasifier Applications

The applications include diversity and can be economically viable too.

Microscale applications

Generally, these gasifier applications gets classified for lower power ranges between 1 – 7 kW. This is the range used by most of the farmers for irrigation purpose in the developing countries.

The equipment must be simple, cheap, light in weight and easily transportable. Ideally, the charcoal gasifiers which are manufactured locally can meet such specific requirements.

Small-scale applications

Generally, these gasifier applications gets classified for power ranges between 7 – 30 kW.

The size of such applications is appropriate for the villages in some developing countries. The cost should be minimal and it should need less maintenance and operations. Also, it should be reliable and economically sustainable. The designs should be simple. Moreover, the gasifiers serving such applications need proper testing.

Medium scale applications

Generally, these gasifier applications gets classified for power ranges between 30 -500 kW.

These applications are widely used in the small to medium agricultural industries and forestry industries. Generally, they are used in sawmills, wood cutting industries, and in generating power. They can be used for supplying power to the remote areas.

The manufacturing, installations can be a bit costly as it requires high equipment and supply of fuels and such matter to the gasifier. Increase in demand for such type of equipment can result in lower productions costs. Also, it can impact the standardization of the parts.

The estimated cost of these applications depends on the type and amount of fuel and extensively on the level of automation. The costs can vary from 300 – 800 US$/kW for the manufactured reactors only, excluding the equipment.

Large-scale applications

Generally, these gasifier applications gets classified for higher power ranges between 500 kW and above. Thus, they are costly and need the utmost care while construction and delivery.

Gasifiers that are costly and highly quipped such as the fixed bed installations serve these applications. The design is complex and thus needs to be developed by specialized construction firms and high engineering. The equipment is fully automated and has high customizations.

Other Gasifier Applications

Most of the gasifiers serve many other purposes such as generation of heat. This high demand and usage are because of the minimal requirements for the tar and moisture content.

As per the high demand of gasifiers and their applications, in future, it can spread across various industries like

- Pulp industries
- Cement industries
- Metallurgy
- Lime industries

Waste to Energy(WTE) for Waste Management

A variety of technologies have been introduced for processing the organic wastes and unused fuels. The Waste to Energy(WTE) Implementations are one such solution that can help the sustainable management of wastes. However, this is still a new technology and a bit complex to implement in various regions.

Advantages of waste to energy

- It is a usable solution in urban and rural areas.

- It reduces the amount of industrial or any waste sent to the landfills.

- It produces energy through the fuel gases with the best utilization of solid and liquid wastes.

- The solution should be financially viable.

- The solution should be feasible with the environmental norms.

Thus, with the increase in the industrial and municipal wastes, there has been a consequent increase in the demand of gasification processes. Moreover, new technologies such as Waste-to-energy also provide environment-friendly solutions for effective waste management and power and thermal generations.

CHAPTER 6

A Wood-Gas Stove for You

The Problem

Since the beginning of civilization wood and biomass have been used for cooking. Over 2 billion people cook badly on inefficient wood stoves that waste wood, cause health problems and destroy the forest. Electricity, gas or liquid fuels are preferred for cooking - when they can be obtained, but they depend on having a suitable infrastructure and are often not available in developing countries. In the last few decades, many improved wood stoves have been developed (the Chula, the Hiko, the

Maendeleo, the Kuni Mbili, etc.), but the new wood stoves are often more difficult to manufacture, often more heat goes to the stove than to the food, and they do not offer good control of cooking rate.

They are not always accepted by the cooks for whom they are developed. Because of the problems of wood cooking, people often cook over charcoal. However, charcoal manufacture is very wasteful of energy and very polluting, so the problems of the wood stove are externalized but not solved.

The Solution

Gas is preferred for cooking wherever it is available. Gas can be made from wood and biomass in gasifiers developed in this century, but these gasifiers are generally too big for home use. A downdraft stove for domestic cooking is now being manufactured in China.

I have developed a new "inverted downdraft gasifier" stove. It operates using only natural convection. The rate of gas production and heating is controlled by the primary air supply to the gasifier. As an option, the gasifier can make charcoal with a 20-25% yield. The wood-gas stove consists of an "inverted downdraft gasifier" (plus a burner to mix air and gas and burn cleanly.

These sections are discussed below. The stove has been started and operated indoors with no exhaust fans and no odor of burning wood. However, I believe that there is still much work to be done in optimizing the stove for various fuels, adapting it to various cooking situations and developing other uses. For that reason I am publishing my preliminary results and hope that others will help adapt these principles to improve world cooking and wood conservation.

Construction of the Wood-Gas Stove

The Inverted Downdraft Gasifier

Wood gasifiers can be classified as: Fixed bed (updraft and downdraft); and fluidized bed. Fluidized bed gasifiers Require high power input, and exact controls and are suitable only for large installations. Updraft gasifiers produce large amounts of tar while consuming the charcoal residue and are not suitable for cooking.

Downdraft gasifiers in the 5-100 kW level were widely used in World War II for operating vehicles and trucks because of the relatively low tar levels.

In operation, air is drawn down through a bed of burning wood, consuming the volatiles. The resulting gas then passes over the resulting charcoal and is reduced to a low energy fuel gas. However, since hot gases naturally rise, it is necessary to supply power to draw the gases DOWN through the gasifier.

In 1985 the "inverted downdraft gasifier" (also called "upside downdraft, or pyrolysing gasifier) was developed and it was operating on natural draft. The name comes from the fact that the fuel charge is lit ON THE TOP, and forms a layer of charcoal there; the flaming pyrolysis zone is below that; the unburned fuel is on the bottom of the pile, and primary air for pyrolytic gasification enters at the bottom and moves UP, forming gas in the flaming pyrolysis zone.

At that time a clean, efficient stove using a jet of compressed air to mix secondary air with the gas and a venturi burner to hold the flame was built.

However, developing country households typically do not have compressed air, so we began development of a natural draft, close coupled cooking gasifier.

In 1991 a cooking stove based on the inverted downdraft gasifier with natural draft secondary air entering the gasifier above the charcoal zone was described.

The combustion in this stove was relatively clean, but the poor air-gas mixing resulted in a unstable, partly yellow flame. The stove is marketed under the name "GAS-I-FIRE".

The inverted downdraft gasifier is operated in batch mode, appropriate for cooking meals. (The gasifier can also be operated continuously by addition of an auger feed for the fuel at the bottom and an auger to remove charcoal at the top. However, this complicates construction.)

Several dozen gasifiers from tin cans, pails, stove pipes and "riser sleeves" has been built. They are gasifiers varying in size from 10 cm (4 in) to 25 cm (10 in) inside diameter. Also, several dozen burner combinations hav been built while looking for clean combustion from the burner. The simplest gasifiers are made from 2 lb coffee cans using a "church key" can opener to punch holes in the bottom. Heat losses are high in can stoves, but they are very simple to build. We use metal shears for cutting the metal parts, and sheet metal screws for outside attachments and burner and pan supports. "Riser sleeves" are particularly useful for construction of these stoves.

They are made for use in casting molten iron and bronze, so are not affected by the temperatures involved in gasification and combustion. They are available in nominal 3 in to 6 in inside diameter in ½ in steps and in 6 to 10 in inside diameter in one-inch steps.

All stock sleeves are 30 cm (12 in) tall. As purchased, they are relatively soft and can be cut with saw or razor knife.

However, they can also be "rigidized" by application of amorphous silica. They provide excellent insulation, and this is particularly important in small diameter gasifiers. 15 cm OD, 12.5 cm ID sleeves 30 cm tall capable of containing molten steel retail for about $3 in the U.S.

I believe that the stove can be built for under US$10 in the U.S. or developing countries. A major advantage of the inverted downdraft gasifier is that the rate of gas production depends on the amount of primary air admitted to the bottom. For this reason it is very important to put a tight sealing valve on the bottom which permits a wide range of air adjustments.

There are also constructions of very satisfactory stoves from tin cans with riser sleeve liners. Use of the outer can permits addition of simple handles to the gasifier and burner sections.

i.   The Wood-Gas Burner

Many burner designs have been tested for the wood-gasifier. The simplest is a series of holes in the gasifier above the level of the charcoal.

However, this does not give good mixing and complete combustion. A better burner consists of a second can mounted a distance of about 1 cm above the first can. Air enters through this annular ring and mixes with the gas and burns.

Conventional gas stoves typically have a ring of fire about 70-120 mm in diameter and about 5 mm across the ring.

ii.   Wood-gas Stove Fuels

Successfully gasified 1-3 cm softwood chips, 1-2 X 10 cm hardwood sticks and 5 mm diameter canes from bushes. The hard woods produce a relatively dense charcoal; the softwoods produce a lighter more friable charcoal.

Much of the tests made on the stove used 2 X 1 X ½ cm air dry (about 7% moisture in Denver) Aspen chips in order to have reproducibility. However, the stove have been found to operate at least as well on sticks standing vertically. Smaller fuel particles do not permit sufficient air to pass through the bed, and so we have not had success gasifying 0.5 mm wood pellets or corn.

iii.   Wood-Gas Stove Operation

The gasifier is filled to within 2 cm of the top. It is desirable to have the fire spread rapidly laterally across the surface to provide gas over the whole area, so an easily combustible material, such as dry pine needles, fibers soaked in animal fat or vegetable grease or other "tinder" is placed on top. The tinder is ignited in several places with a match and allowed to burn for a minute or so. When a stable flame is established all around, the burner is placed slowly on top of the gasifier to permit the inside surfaces to become hot. A continuous (smokeless) blue flame was established in 2 minutes and ran continuously for 37 minutes when it went out in Run.

The weight of stove (plus the change of weight of 1 liter of water in a pan, added at minute 11). It is seen that the stove burned about 12 g/min with full primary air. At 20 min primary air was turned to 20 % and the stove then burned at a rate of 4.5 g/min. 155 g of charcoal remained at the end of the run.

iv.   **Wood-gas stove emissions**

Wood-gas cooking has very low emissions and can be operated indoors with proper precautions once established. However, if the fire is extinguished for any reason the production of smoke and CO continues, so that it is important to be able to extinguish it completely or take it outside. The stove is difficult to extinguish and the bottom air valve must be AIR TIGHT. A pan of water can then be placed on top of the gasifier and there will be no subsequent production of smoke. In a preliminary measurement we have measured the CO level 80 cm above the stove as 22 PPM. The level in the room had no measurable rise. During gasification of wood, if the fire is extinguished the acrid tars in the wood make it unlikely that one would breathe too much CO. However, after the wood is gasified the stove contains hot charcoal and so can be a major source of CO. For this reason it is important to either continue to burn the charcoal or to cut off ALL air to the stove and preserve the charcoal as discussed below.

v.   Charcoal manufacture

In a typical run we have a charcoal yield of 10-15% (dry basis). If it is desired to keep the charcoal, it is important that it be possible to close off ALL air to the charcoal after the volatiles are consumed. The valve should be made of relatively stiff metal to permit a tight closure. The top of the gasifier is closed with a pan over the top. In addition it is useful to spray water on the top pan and the lower parts of the stove to cool it down to prevent continuing oxidation of the charcoal.

vi.   Stove Testing

Fuel consumption in most of the development runs on the stove were monitored by placing the stove, chimney-burner etc. on a digital balance and recording the weight every minute during the run. In this way it was possible to determine the rate of consumption as a function of primary air setting.

A mass-energy balance was made in a small gasifier connected to a flowmeter and an integrating total flow (Singer) meter. The flow was fixed at 10 scfh from 3 to 30 minutes. The gas was burned in a 10-15 cm high diffusion flame above the gasifier. 135 g of aspen chips 7.8% moisture produced 26.3 g of charcoal (yield =19.5%, 24.2% dry basis). The total air flow was 160 g of air or 30.8 g O2. The mass and energy balances are then:

The air/fuel ratio is 1.28. The air/fuel ratio for complete combustion is 6.36, so the equivalence ratio (air consumed/air required for complete combustion) for this test is 0.20 (compared to .25 for equilibrium gasification of dry wood. The gas probably has a higher energy content than conventional gas because no air is required for char conversion. The hat gas energy content will be particularly high because it contains the sensible heat and volatiles as well as the gas.

vii.   Preliminary Modelling of The Wood-Gas Stove

A major advantage of the wood-gas stove is that the gasifier section is stratified and so can be modeled using a simple one dimensional flow scheme. We modeled the conventional stratified downdraft gasifier ("open-top" gasifier, "topless gasifier") and are using the same approach for the inverted downdraft gasifier. The following guidelines are useful for predicting fuel consumption, burn time, stove power and stove size.

Power: The heat content of the gas is ~ 18kJ/g, so consumption of 4-10 g/m produces 1.2-3.0 kWt. (U.S. Electric stoves usually have a 1.5 and a 2.5 kW burner.).

The production rate is approximately proportional to cross sectional area. Larger cooking jobs will require larger stoves

Primary Air: The heat for pyrolysis is about 2,000 j/g. Pyrolysis requires 2/3 g air/per g wood or 600 ml air/g wood. 3 kWt requires 6 l air/min

Primary draft: The pyrolysis gas temperature is about 500 °C and so generates a draft of 100 mm-water pressure

Secondary draft: The gas flow around the gas wick is quite complex and work is in progress on calculation of the gas and air flow

The wood-gas stove has been started and operated indoors with no exhaust fans and no odor of burning wood. However, we believe that there is still much work to be done in optimizing the stove for various fuels, determining the effect of moisture, adapting it to various cooking situations and developing other uses. For that reason we are publishing our preliminary results here and hope that others will help adapt these principles to improve world cooking and wood conservation.

CHAPTER 7

How to Make Your Own Gasifier Stove

The design of this 'wood gasifier' stove is exceedingly simple and it can be built in under an hour using only empty tin cans and a few very basic tools.

It would make a great little maker project with your kids; you'll have great fun working on building this together, and will have a superb little cooking stove to use afterwards! The gasifier design is also a wonderfully compact and efficient stove, burning twigs you can collect yourself (rather than gas canisters), that's ideal for cooking during a barbecue in the back garden or even on a family camping trip.

The gasifier stove is made up of a smaller can nestled inside a larger can, allowing air to circulate in the gap between them. Wood is loaded into the inner can as fuel, and as it burns it draws fresh air up through the bottom for a hearty, intense combustion – just like any barbecue. What's unique about a gasifier stove is that it has a second, higher row of air holes that reintroduce oxygen. As wood breaks down in the heat of a fire it releases lots of gases and vapours and smoke that are all actually flammable, but would otherwise have blown away in a normal fire.

But with this second row of air holes, fresh oxygen is drawn in and you get secondary combustion of all these gases. This means a gasifier stove is very efficient and releases all of the heat energy in the fuel, and is also smokeless when it's running. Gasification of wood has been crucial through history, and can even be used to drive a car or van instead of petrol or diesel – there were over a million wood-powered cars across Europe during the Second World War!

Here's how to make your own gasifier stove.

You will need:

- one large can (the size of a normal paint tin)
- three normal-sized cans (the size of an average baked bean tin)
- drill
- small metal shears
- file
- kitchen tongs

What to do:

1. Remove the bottom of the large can, and empty out the contents. If you don't have a can opener, see this neat trick here on how to open a can without using any tools.
2. Drill a row or two of large holes around the bottom of the large can.

3. Cut out a circular hole in the centre of the top of the large can, the same size as the normal-sized can. You can use the base of the smaller can as a template and etch (or use a marker pen) around the outline. You'll find it easier if you drill a few holes just inside the outline and then use the metal cutting shears to snip around the circle.

4. Remove the top of one of the normal-sized cans. Drill plenty of holes into the bottom of the can. Also drill a row of holes about half an inch from the top of the can.

5. Use the file to take off any sharp edges or burrs in both cans.

6. Now carefully ease the smaller can down through the snug hole in the top of the larger can, as shown in the picture, so that you have one can nestled within each another. The top rim of the small can should be flush with the top surface of the big can, so that holes on the bottom are held suspended in the air.

7. Load up the inner can with some kindling (dry newspaper will work a treat) and just a small handful of twigs, broken into little pieces, and filling no higher than about half-way up the inner can.

8. You can help the stove get started by adding a flue on top of the combustion can, to encourage a strong updraft of air through the fire. Make a flue from a few extra cans and taking off both tops and bottoms. You can slot them together into a hollow tube about a foot long by snipping a short cut into the top of one can so that it can be squeezed slightly and slotted into the bottom of the next can.

Light the kindling in your gasifier stove through the air holes at the bottom, and be amazed at how quickly it gets going. You have a roaring fire to either cook with, or simply sit around in the evening!